GDPR for HR Professionals

By Daniel Barnett and Emma Erskine-Fox

3rd Edition

The Employment Law Library

All books in the Employment Law Library are sent for free to members of the HR Inner Circle.

1. Employee Investigations
2. GDPR for HR Professionals
3. Preventing and Defending Employee Stress Claims
4. Employment Tribunal Time Limits
5. Deconstructing TUPE
6. Changing Terms & Conditions
7. Constructive Dismissal
8. Resolving Grievances
9. HR Hazards
10. Employment Status
11. Spotting Malingering
12. Employment Tribunal Compensation
13. Hiring Staff
14. Computer and Social Media Misuse
15. Managing Sickness Absence
16. The Three Ps
17. Conflict at Work
18. SOSR Dismissals
19. Dismissing Problem Employees
20. Menopause and the Workplace
21. Dismissing Senior Executives
22. Negotiating Exit Packages and Settlement Agreements

Published by HR Inner Circle Limited, Unit 3, Chequers Farm, Chequers Lane, Watford, Hertfordshire WD25 0LG

DANIEL BARNETT
BARRISTER

HOME ~~~~ PLAYLISTS   COMMUNITY   CHANNELS   ABOUT

Try these f...

CAN PRESIDENT TRUMP PARDON HIMSELF?
...Trump

HELP I'M BEING BULLIED AT WORK 13:45
Help - I'm being bullied at work: a practical guide for...
Daniel Barnett
4.5K views • 3 weeks ago

The most heartbreaking, emotional call I've ever take...
Daniel Barnett
1.2K views • 3 weeks ago

HOW TO HANDLE DISCIPLINARY DISMISSAL AND PERFORMANCE MANAGEMENT SITUAT 1:53:34
How to Handle Disciplinary, Dismissal and Performance...
Daniel Barnett
688 views • 1 month ago

ASK THE PRESIDENT EMPLOYMENT TRIBUNALS PRESIDENT (E&W) JUDGE BARRY CLARKE 1:13:52
...k the President: Judge ...ry Clarke, President of...
Daniel Barnett
...k views • 2 weeks ago

FAIRNESS IN REDUNDANCY SELECTION REBECCA TUCK QC 44:01
Fair Redundancy Dismissals with Rebecca Tuck QC
Daniel Barnett
1K views • 2 weeks ago

HELP I'M BEING BULLIED AT WORK 13:45
Help - I'm being bullied at work: a practical guide for...
Daniel Barnett
4.5K views • 3 weeks ago

THE UK'S LEADING YOUTUBE CHANNEL FOR LAW EXPLAINER VIDEOS

BIT.LY/YOUTUBELEGAL

About the Authors

Daniel Barnett is an employment law barrister, practising from Chambers in London. He is the founder of the HR Inner Circle, one of the leading trainers on UK employment law, and presents the Legal Hour on LBC Radio.

Emma Erskine-Fox is a partner at national law firm TLT, specialising in Data and AI. She is well-known as an expert in her field, having been included in The Lawyer's coveted Hot 100 list in 2025. She advises clients on all aspects of data, privacy and cybersecurity law, as well as compliance with AI law and regulation.

Acknowledgments

Thank you to Claire Scott for her help with researching the first edition of this book.

Thank you also to Aaron Gaff, Tincuta Collett and Maria Rodriguez for their help with the editing and publishing process.

None of these books are possible without the input and experience of the members of the HR Inner Circle – thanks to all of you.

Finally, Emma Erskine-Fox would like to thank Daniel Barnett for the opportunity to contribute to this updated third edition, and her other team partners and colleagues at TLT whose insight, energy and friendship keep her enthusiasm for data protection alive and well. Emma is particularly grateful to fellow partner Ed Hayes for casting a reassuring second pair of eyes over her draft.

Daniel Barnett

2025

Table of Contents

Introduction

The UK's data protection regime and why it's important

D ata protection may not set pulses racing, yet it is fundamental to good governance and can quickly become complex. Its reach extends far beyond HR into every aspect of running an organisation.

This book aims to keep things practical and easy to follow, while also providing the background you need to understand your obligations.

First, the basics. In the UK, the two key laws to know are the *United Kingdom General Data Protection Regulation* (UK GDPR) and the *Data Protection Act 2018.*

The UK GDPR is based on an EU law that came into effect in May 2018. After the UK left the EU, the GDPR was kept in UK law, with modifications to make it effective within the UK legal framework. It operates alongside the *Data Protection Act 2018* (often shortened to the DPA), which supports the UK GDPR by adding more detail. For example, the DPA sets out conditions for processing special category and criminal offence data; introduces some exemptions; and creates a few criminal offences, such as accessing or sharing personal data without permission.

The legal framework is supported by guidance from the Information Commissioner's Office (ICO), which regulates data protection in the UK. The ICO publishes helpful material on many areas, including HR-specific issues like employee monitoring, recruitment, records and mental health emergencies. This is a good starting point for best practice.

At the time of writing (July 2025), the Data (Use and Access) Act ('DUA Act') has received royal assent. The DUA Act doesn't overhaul the system, but it does make changes, especially around automated decision-making. The changes will be phased in between June 2025 and June 2026, and throughout this book, we have made it clear where the DUA Act alters current rules.

Do we still need to think about the EU GDPR?

In many cases, yes. If your organisation operates in both the UK and the EU, or if you provide goods or services to people in the EU or monitor EU nationals, you may need to comply with both the UK and EU GDPR.

Right now, the UK and EU rules are almost identical, so complying with one usually means you're complying with the other. But when the DUA Act is fully implemented, some small differences will emerge. Most of these changes are technical and unlikely to impact day-to-day operations significantly. Many organisations will still find it easier to apply a single high standard across all countries rather than running different rules for different regions.

What happens if you get it wrong?

Data protection is now a board-level issue. That's because the consequences of non-compliance have become far more serious since the implementation of the GDPR.

The biggest concern for most businesses is the risk of fines. Before 2018, the ICO could issue a maximum fine of £500,000. Now, the maximum is £17.5 million or 4% of global annual turnover, whichever is higher.

But financial penalties aren't the only risk. The ICO has other powers too. It can issue enforcement notices, order audits, and require you to stop or change certain practices. In February 2024, the ICO issued an enforcement notice against Serco after it used facial recognition technology to monitor staff attendance. The ICO required Serco to stop using the system and delete the data it had collected. Even though there was no fine, the company still faced major disruption and costs.

The ICO can also issue public reprimands. These do not carry a fine, or any other strict legal consequences, but can cause reputational damage.

There are also criminal offences under the DPA. These include accessing or sharing data without permission, or deleting or changing data to avoid disclosing it in response to a subject access request. There are some defences, such as having a reasonable belief that you had permission or were legally entitled to act. Deleting data as part of normal retention processes isn't a criminal offence even if a subject access request is in progress.

Data breaches regularly make headlines, and reputational harm can be significant. Individuals also have the right to claim compensation if their data is mishandled. This can cover financial loss and non-financial harm, such as distress.

How does data protection law affect employers?

Data protection applies across all areas of business that handle personal data, including customers, suppliers and users. But it also applies to personal data about your staff.

This book uses the term 'employees' to cover all categories, including workers, consultants and other similar groups.

Employers routinely process large amounts of personal data for many reasons, such as:

- Background checks
- Payroll and benefits
- Insurance
- Performance reviews
- Attendance monitoring
- Disciplinaries and grievances
- Diversity monitoring
- Training
- Meeting legal obligations

The types of personal data can be very broad, and may include:

- Financial, personal and health information
- Details about ethnicity or religion
- CVs and performance records
- Information in emails, messages, CCTV footage or interview notes

In addition, the data is not always just about the employee. For example, if an employee emails their manager to say their child has a rash and needs to see a doctor, that contains personal data about the child. This may also be special category data, which has extra protections under the law.

In large organisations, compliance is often managed by legal or compliance teams, with input from HR and IT. In smaller businesses, though, responsibility often sits squarely with HR.

So, what do you need to know, and what do you need to do? That's what this book is here to help with.

Chapter 1

Overview of important concepts and principles

The UK GDPR is built around a set of key principles for processing personal data. One of these is the principle of accountability, which means you must be able to demonstrate how your organisation complies with the rules.

Before exploring how this applies to HR, it's worth setting out a few core concepts and definitions.

Personal data means any information that relates to a living person who can be identified from that information, either on its own or combined with other data you hold. This includes things like names, addresses, contact details, employment and financial records, disciplinary notes, appraisals and health records.

It also includes opinions about someone and any indication of what you intend to do in relation to them.

For example, if a manager emails HR to say they are thinking of placing an employee on a performance plan, that email is personal data about the employee.

A more sensitive type of personal data is known as **special category data**. This includes information about:

- Race or ethnic origin
- Religion, philosophical beliefs or political opinions
- Trade union membership
- Health
- Genetic or biometric data
- Sexual orientation or sex life

This type of data is given extra protection under the UK GDPR, and stricter conditions apply before you can use it.

The term **processing** refers to almost anything you do with personal data. It includes collecting, storing, organising, amending, sharing or deleting data.

There is also a key legal distinction between a **controller** and a **processor**.

A **controller** is the entity that decides why and how personal data is used. Most employers are controllers in respect of their employees' data.

A **processor** acts only on the controller's instructions and does not decide how the data will be used. Examples include external payroll providers, cloud-based HR systems or IT services. Sometimes, one company in a group may act as a processor on behalf of another – for example, if it provides centralised admin support or hosts shared systems. Whether the recipient is another controller or a processor affects your responsibilities when sharing data, which is explored further in Chapter 6.

The data protection principles

The UK GDPR sets out six key principles for processing personal data:

1. Process data lawfully, fairly and transparently.

2. Collect and use data only for specific, legitimate purposes.

3. Only process data that is relevant, adequate and limited to what is necessary.

4. Keep personal data accurate and up to date.

5. Don't keep personal data longer than necessary.

6. Keep personal data secure and confidential.

Alongside these sits a seventh principle: **accountability.** This requires you not only to follow the rules but also to be able to show you're doing so. That means having appropriate policies, internal processes and staff awareness in place. Written policies alone aren't enough; your team must know what they need to do in practice.

Linked to this is a duty to keep records of your data processing activities. These should include retention periods, any international data transfers and details of who receives the data. The ICO can ask to see these records at any time.

Other key obligations under the UK GDPR include:

- **Data subject rights:** Individuals have a range of rights in relation to their personal data, such as access, correction and deletion. Some are rarely used, like the right to restrict processing, but you still need to be ready to respond appropriately if someone exercises them. See Chapter 5 for more detail.

- **Data protection by design and by default:** You must think about data protection from the outset of any project or new processing activity, not bolt it on afterwards. In some cases, this includes carrying out a Data Protection Impact Assessment (DPIA), particularly where the processing involves high risks. This is covered in Chapter 4.

- **International transfers:** If you send personal data outside the UK, special rules apply. Transfers to countries with an 'adequacy decision', such as those in the EEA, can go ahead freely. For other destinations, you need to put safeguards in place, like standard contractual clauses. There's more on this in Chapter 6.

With the key definitions and principles covered, the following chapters will explore how these obligations play out in day-to-day HR practice – and how you can ensure your data processing remains lawful and well managed.

Chapter 2

Lawful basis for processing personal data

A core requirement of data protection law, and a key part of the first principle (Process data lawfully, fairly and transparently), is that you must have a lawful basis for processing personal data.

Many people assume that consent is always needed. In fact, it is just one of six possible lawful bases, and in an HR context, it is usually best avoided. We will explain why later.

For each processing activity, you must identify and record the specific lawful basis you are relying on. It is not enough to say, "employee data" or "HR processing". Different activities, such as running payroll or conducting diversity monitoring, may require different legal justifications.

The six lawful bases under the UK GDPR are:

1. The employee has given consent to the processing.

2. The processing is necessary for the performance of a contract with the employee, or to take steps at their request before entering into a contract.

3. The processing is necessary to comply with a legal obligation.

4. The processing is necessary to protect someone's vital interests, typically in a life-or-death scenario.

5. The processing is necessary for a task carried out in the public interest.

6. The processing is necessary for the legitimate interests of the employer or a third party, provided those interests are not overridden by the rights and freedoms of the individual.

Each of these lawful bases is explored in more detail in the following sections, including when they can be used, examples of when they might apply in an employment context, and why consent is rarely the right choice in practice.

Consent

Consent under the UK GDPR has a high standard: it must be "freely given, specific, informed and unambiguous" and shown through a clear, positive action.

In an employment setting, it's hard to meet this standard. That's because there's a power imbalance – the employer is in control, and the employee may feel they have no real choice but to agree if they want to keep or get the job. That makes it difficult to prove that consent is truly "freely given".

Consent must also be "specific", meaning you need to explain and get agreement for each separate purpose – which is impractical and confusing.

It also has to be "separate" from other documents – not hidden in the contract or other policies. And withdrawing consent must be just as easy as giving it. Asking for consent when you plan to process the data anyway can be misleading, especially if employees can't realistically say no or change their minds later.

It used to be common to include a consent clause in employment contracts, but most employers have stopped doing this.

You might still be able to rely on consent in very limited cases – but only if employees are told clearly that they can say no without any negative consequences. A real, free choice is essential.

That said, in most cases, you'll be able to rely on one of the other lawful grounds for processing employee data, so you probably won't need to use consent (see below for exceptions relating to special category data).

Contractual necessity

This is a useful legal basis for employers. It lets you process personal data when it's needed to carry out a contract – either with the employee or with someone else on their behalf.

Most day-to-day data use at work fits here – like processing payroll or holiday requests – because it's required to deliver what's promised in the employment contract.

But there are two key things to remember:

1. **It only covers your obligations** – not the employee's. For example, you can't use this to justify collecting access card data to check whether employees are coming into the office as required by their contract. That's about monitoring them, not delivering your side of the contract. Similarly, using data during a disciplinary process might not count. You may have a right to investigate, but unless your contract requires you to run a disciplinary process, it doesn't qualify as a contractual obligation.

2. **It must be necessary and proportionate.** The ICO says data processing must be targeted and not excessive. If there's a less intrusive way to achieve the same goal, this basis may not apply. For instance, using fingerprint scanners to record

attendance might seem justifiable for payroll, but if access cards can do the job with less intrusion, this processing may not be allowed under this ground.

In short, contractual necessity works well for routine employment-related tasks in connection with your contractual obligations as an employer – but for anything beyond that, you'll need to consider other legal bases.

Compliance with a legal obligation

You can use this basis when complying with the law requires you to process personal data. This means a specific legal duty set out in legislation, case law or a court or tribunal order.

It's useful in situations like:

- Giving employee data to HMRC for tax purposes
- Complying with court or tribunal disclosure requests
- Meeting legal duties under health and safety laws
- Following rules like the *Working Time Regulations 1998*
- Paying statutory maternity or sick pay

This legal basis doesn't cover everything, but it does apply to some key areas of employment-related data processing.

Vital interests

This legal basis is only for emergencies. According to ICO guidance, you can only use it when data processing is necessary to protect someone's life.

For example, if an employee collapses at work and you share their known medical history with attending paramedics so they can administer appropriate treatment, the disclosure falls within the vital interests basis.

But in general, this basis won't apply to most workplace situations.

Public task

This lawful basis is unlikely to be applicable for the large majority of employment data processing. It allows processing of personal data where necessary for the performance of a task in the public interest. Whilst there is nothing restricting this to public bodies, it's difficult to show that processing employee data for HR purposes is necessary for a task in the public interest.

Legitimate interests

This is one of the most commonly-used lawful bases, especially for employers. It's often very useful – but you should always consider other options first, as this one comes with extra requirements.

You can rely on this basis when you need to process personal data for your own interests (or someone else's) as long as those interests aren't outweighed by the employee's rights or freedoms.

To use it properly, you need to carry out and document a **legitimate interests assessment** (LIA). This involves three key steps:

1. **Identify the legitimate interest:** What's the purpose of the processing? What benefit does it bring to you, a third party or even society more broadly? What would happen if you couldn't process the data?

2. **Consider whether the data processing is necessary:** Could you achieve the same result in a less intrusive way? If so, this basis might not apply. The processing must be proportionate to the aim.

3. **Balance your interests with the employee's rights:** Would the employee expect this processing? Could it cause harm? If their rights and freedoms outweigh your interest, then you can't use this basis.

The DUA Act introduces a concept of 'recognised legitimate interests', which includes situations where processing is necessary to respond to an emergency or to safeguard vulnerable people. Once the DUA Act is fully implemented, if one of these applies, you won't need to carry out the third step above (i.e. the balancing test).

Two final things to keep in mind:

1. You must **tell employees what your legitimate interests are** – for example, "to run the business efficiently" or "to meet a customer contract".

2. Employees have the right to **object**. If they do, you can only keep processing the data if you can show that your interest is stronger than theirs. If you haven't clearly explained your interests in a privacy notice, it'll be hard to defend your position – and you may have to stop processing. This issue is explored more closely in Chapter 5.

Processing conditions for special category personal data

When you're processing special category personal data (like health, race, religion or sexual orientation), you need two things:

1. A lawful basis (i.e. one of the ones already covered)

2. An additional condition under Article 9 of the UK GDPR that allows this type of sensitive data to be processed.

Some of the key conditions you can rely on include:

- **Explicit consent:** The employee has clearly and specifically agreed to the processing.

- **Public information:** The employee has clearly made the data public, for example, by posting it on a public social media profile.

- **Employment law obligations:** This is often the most useful. It covers legal duties under laws like health and safety, equality, maternity rights, sick pay and TUPE. But it must be a legal duty (set out in statute or case law), not just something in the employment contract. You should clearly record which legal obligation you're relying on.

- **Legal claims:** You're using the data to bring, defend or prepare for a legal claim.

- **Vital interests:** The employee (or someone else) is in danger and can't give consent, for example, in a medical emergency.

- **Health assessments:** A qualified health professional is assessing the employee's ability to work, such as via occupational health.

There are other public interest reasons too, for example, processing data to prevent crime, collect tax or monitor diversity and equality. These aren't always needed, but it's useful to know they're available in certain situations.

Chapter 3

Transparency and other key obligations

Providing information to individuals

Under data protection law, you must give people clear information about how you will use their personal data. This is usually done through a privacy notice.

In the past, employers sometimes included this information in the employment contract. But that's not ideal. It's better to keep the privacy notice as a separate document. That way, you avoid linking it to consent (which can cause problems), and you won't need to update contracts every time your data processing changes.

You must give the privacy notice when you first collect the data, or within one month if you get the data from someone else, such as a recruiter. You can include it in job application packs or induction materials, or you can provide a link to it on your intranet or website; just make sure that individuals are given the link within the timescales above.

A privacy notice is for information only. Employees don't need to agree to it. However, it's a good idea to ask them to confirm they've read it so you have a record for legal compliance. Just make sure you're not asking them to approve or accept it.

Finally, the privacy notice must be clear, easy to access and written in plain language. This can be tricky, given how much information it must contain, but it's important to keep it simple and avoid legal jargon.

So, what do you actually have to tell employees about your processing of their data? It's not a short list; the UK GDPR sets out that you must tell the employee:

- The identity of the data controller (this will be the employer) and your data protection officer, if you have one.

- The purpose(s) of the processing and the lawful basis you are relying on for each purpose.

- If you are relying on "legitimate interests", as mentioned, you need to specify the interest(s) you have identified.

- The source and category of any data you've obtained from a source other than the employee.

- Who you will share personal data with – this doesn't necessarily need to be the names of recipients. It is enough to state the categories of recipients who will receive it, for example, your payroll provider or the company's occupational health provider.

- The period the data will be stored for – if that's not possible, though, you need to tell the employee the criteria you will use to work out the period, for example, during the person's employment and for three years following termination of employment.

- What rights they have over their personal data (these are explored in more detail in Chapter 5).

- The fact that they have the right to withdraw consent, if consent is being relied upon as a legal basis for processing (though, as explained, consent is usually best avoided in an HR context).

- The fact that they have the right to complain to the ICO if they are unhappy with how you have processed their data.

- If the data is going to be transferred to a country outside the UK, including the safeguards in place (see Chapter 6 for more detail on these).

- If you are carrying out any wholly automated decision-making that has a significant effect on the employee (see Chapter 5 for more).

Data protection officers

Data protection officers (DPOs) are required in some situations, though not all employers need one.

You must appoint a DPO if you are a public authority or if your main business activities involve monitoring people or processing large amounts of special category personal data. For example, if you track user behaviour online or work in financial services or a regulated sector, you are likely to need a DPO.

If you're an employer who only processes special category data for standard HR purposes, that alone doesn't mean you need a DPO. Unless you're doing large-scale or high-risk processing, you're unlikely to fall under the mandatory requirement.

That said, some organisations choose to appoint a DPO voluntarily, or they assign similar responsibilities to a Data Protection Manager. If you do this, be aware that DPOs have specific legal protections and duties. They must report to senior management; avoid any conflicts of interest; and have enough experience, training and resources to do the job properly. They are also protected from unfair dismissal.

The DPO's main job is to help you stay compliant with data protection law. They also act as the contact point for both the ICO and individuals whose data is being processed.

Even if you don't need a DPO right now, it's a good idea to review this from time to time, especially if your data processing increases or changes.

Data protection impact assessments

It's also worth briefly mentioning data protection impact assessments (DPIAs). These are risk assessments that help you identify and manage potential data protection issues before starting new ways of processing personal data.

A well-run DPIA is more than a compliance box-tick. It is an early warning system that forces the project team to pause, articulate precisely what data will flow and judge whether the intended gains justify the privacy impacts. A practical sequence for HR projects could be:

1. Describe the initiative in plain language that the board can understand. For example, "roll out facial recognition terminals to replace security passes at three UK sites".

2. Map every data element that will be collected, created or inferred, and record who inside and outside the organisation will see it.

3. Assess proportionality by asking whether the same business objective (say, accurate time and attendance records) could be achieved by a less intrusive option, such as proximity cards or random spot checks.

4. Having established necessity, analyse risks to individuals. Use a simple matrix, rating each risk by likelihood and severity and referencing concrete scenarios, such as a misplaced enrolment tablet, biased algorithms rejecting a disabled employee or system downtime blocking site access. For each risk, identify mitigations, assign owners and record residual risk.

5. Involve your DPO, IT security and, if relevant, the recognised union or employee forum. Their feedback should be folded back into the DPIA, creating an auditable trail.

6. The final steps are sign-off by a senior accountable owner, dissemination of key findings to the workforce and diarising a review (usually six or 12 months after go-live) to confirm assumptions remain valid.

By treating the DPIA as living documentation rather than a static PDF, HR gains a credible defence if the ICO questions the project, and an internal playbook for repeatable privacy-by-design practice.

If you work in a larger organisation, you may already be familiar with DPIAs. Sometimes, they are required by law, and even when they're not, they can still be very useful. The ICO recommends using DPIAs and provides helpful guidance and a template to follow.

Under the UK GDPR, you must carry out a DPIA if data processing is likely to result in a high risk to people's rights and freedoms. This is especially important when using new technologies.

Whether processing is high risk depends on the situation, but it could include:

- Automated decision-making or profiling that has legal or significant effects on people (such as AI-based decisions)

- Analysing or predicting someone's work performance, health, behaviour, finances, preferences or location

- Large-scale or regular monitoring, such as CCTV in public spaces or the processing of criminal conviction data

In HR, DPIAs may be mandatory if you:

- Introduce AI tools to screen job applications

- Switch to biometric ID for clocking in and out

- Use access card data to track office attendance

The ICO has more examples on its website. Even if you decide a DPIA is not legally required, it may still be a good idea to use one, especially for new or sensitive projects.

Breaches of security

We've all seen examples of data security breaches. It could be sending an email to the wrong person, misplacing a memory stick or leaving a laptop on public transport. These things often happen by accident, though deliberate breaches can occur too – for example, in the Morrisons case, where an employee with a grudge uploaded the personal data of 100,000 colleagues online. The Supreme Court decided Morrisons wasn't legally responsible for his actions, but the incident still caused major disruption.

If a personal data breach is likely to pose a risk to someone's rights or freedoms, you must report it to the ICO promptly, and within 72 hours if possible. This is a strict deadline measured in calendar hours – weekends and bank holidays don't pause the clock. The countdown starts from the point when someone in your organisation has "reasonable certainty" that a breach has happened. If you report the breach late, you'll need to explain why.

You don't have to report a breach if there's no risk to individuals – for example, if the data was encrypted and can't be read by anyone who finds it. But if people could face identity theft, emotional distress or other harm, then there is a risk, and the breach should be reported.

When notifying the ICO, you must explain what happened, how many people might be affected, what the likely consequences are and what steps you've taken or plan to take. If the breach poses a high risk to individuals, you must also tell the people affected directly.

You must keep a record of all personal data breaches, even if you don't need to tell the ICO or the individuals affected. This includes what happened and what action you took in response.

Breaches can range from large incidents, like the Morrisons case, to smaller mistakes, for example, using CC instead of BCC in an email, or sending personal data to the wrong email address.

Because there's a strict 72-hour deadline for reporting certain breaches to the ICO, it's essential that all employees can recognise what counts as a personal data breach and know what to do if one occurs. Everyone should understand the urgency and who to report it to, so having clear internal procedures is crucial.

- Establish a response blueprint that mirrors the way HR already deals with other workplace incidents so that people recognise the pattern under pressure. This response blueprint could, for example, look something like this:

- The moment a breach is suspected, the employee who has discovered it must log key facts in plain language: what happened, when and which systems and people might be affected.

- This note should go straight to a dedicated mailbox that alerts HR, IT security, legal and the DPO at once. Those key stakeholders are responsible for deciding whether the incident meets the definition of a personal data breach and setting a provisional severity rating, drawn from the organisation's risk matrix.

Once that decision has been made, various different work streams run in parallel:

* **Containment:** focussing on stopping the breach, securing evidence and taking other steps to mitigate the impact of the breach on employees.

* **Assessment:** verifying which data fields left the organisation and whose they were.

* **Remediation:** addressing the root cause of the breach and taking steps to remedy the issue. Common actions include forced password resets, accelerated encryption projects or refresher training for the function/ staff member(s) involved.

* **Communication:** if required, drafting the ICO notification and any staff or customer messages.

* **Documentation:** maintaining the timeline, collecting screenshots, emails and decisions to satisfy later audit or litigation, if necessary.

- An incident manager (this could be someone in HR with crisis-management experience) should keep the timetable up front so the 72-hour ICO deadline is never lost in the detail.

- The final step is a 'lessons learned' report, signed off by a senior executive sponsor, and ensure that the agreed improvements are entered into the risk register and revisited three months later. Treating breach response as an iterative cycle rather than a one-off event helps embed a culture of continuous learning around data security.

It's also important to create a culture where people feel safe reporting mistakes. If staff are worried about being blamed, they may try to hide breaches instead of reporting them, which only makes the situation worse.

Data retention

Turning the fifth data protection principle (don't keep personal data longer than necessary) into practice isn't always easy, but it starts with a retention schedule that everyone can follow without legal training.

Begin by grouping HR records into natural life-cycle phases, such as recruitment, active employment, post-employment and litigation hold. For each group, list any statutory minimum or maximum retention periods that already exist – for example, there is a minimum retention period of three years for health and safety training records under the *Management of Health and Safety at Work Regulations 1999*, and the *Limitation Act 1980* specifies certain periods after which a claim cannot be brought, meaning it is often sensible to link retention periods for relevant documents to that Act.

Where no statute applies, agree a pragmatic period that balances business needs and employee expectations, then document the business rationale in a plain English sentence so future reviewers understand why the figure was chosen.

Next, build triggers that move records through those phases automatically. If you use a modern Human Resource Information System, configure it to flag files that reach 90% of their retention limit so owners can review them and either justify extension or approve deletion. Where systems lack automation, schedule a quarterly report that lists records by age and owner, making the business accountable for timely disposal.

Deletion need not mean immediate erasure from every backup. A two-stage approach often works best:

1. remove the data from live systems so it is no longer searchable; and,

2. then allow routine backup rotation to overwrite it.

Keep a short record of what was deleted and when, both for audit and to defend any future claims that data was destroyed selectively. Publish the schedule on the intranet beside the privacy notice so employees can see at a glance how long different categories of information will be kept and why.

Chapter 4

The rights of employees as data subjects

All individuals, including employees, have specific rights over their personal data under the UK GDPR. These rights include:

- The right to be informed about how their personal data is being used

- The right to access their personal data (this is often called a data subject access request, and is familiar to many HR professionals)

- The right to correct personal data if it is wrong

- The right to have personal data deleted in some cases (often referred to as the right to be forgotten)

- The right to limit how their data is used in certain situations

- The right to object to data processing when it is based on legitimate interests

- The right to receive their personal data in a digital format or transfer it to another organisation (this is called data portability)

- The right not to be subject to decisions made only by automated systems that have legal or significant effects, except in limited circumstances

You usually have to respond to any of the rights listed above without unnecessary delay, and within one month at the latest.

In some cases, you can extend the time limit by up to two more months, giving you a total of three months to respond. Such extensions are only allowed if the request is complex or if the person has made several requests at the same time.

Data subject access requests

The most common right employees use under data protection law is the right of subject access. These requests are usually called data subject access requests (DSARs). Some people also refer to them as SARs, but that term can be confusing in some industries, such as financial services, where it also refers to suspicious activity reports.

So, what is a DSAR, and when do you have to respond?

1. An employee making a DSAR is entitled to two things:

2. A copy of the personal data you hold about them

Information about how you process that data

You can often meet the second part by giving them a copy of your privacy notice, if you are confident that it covers everything required.

The deadline for responding is one calendar month from the date you receive the request. There is no pause for weekends or bank holidays, and February gives you fewer days to respond than other months. You can extend this deadline by up to two more months if the request is complex or if the employee has made multiple requests at once. But this is not automatic. You must look at each case individually, and the ICO has said that the fact there are a lot of documents is not enough on its own to justify the extension.

Your organisation's size and resources can be relevant. For example, if a small employer receives a DSAR during a legal dispute and has to seek legal advice, the extra time might be justified.

Even with an extension, DSARs can be demanding. You may need to review thousands of documents. That's why it is important that staff are trained to spot a DSAR and escalate it immediately. DSARs can be made in any format, including verbally or via social media. They do not need to use specific language or mention the words "data subject access request" to be valid.

DSARs are increasingly being made in the context of employment disputes. Employers often wonder if the real aim is to gain an advantage in a legal claim. But the ICO's position is clear: the reason behind the request does not matter. If a valid DSAR is made, you must respond. That said, courts sometimes take a stricter view. In *Lees v Lloyds Bank plc [2020] EWHC 2249*, for example, the judge said he would not have ordered disclosure where the request seemed to be about getting documents, not personal data.

In rare cases, you can refuse to respond or charge a reasonable fee if the request is clearly unfounded or excessive. You must explain this to the employee and inform them of their right to complain to the ICO. But be cautious: the bar for this is high. It might apply where someone keeps repeating the same request, or where they suggest dropping the request in exchange for a benefit.

Handling the request

There are a few important things to keep in mind when handling and responding to a DSAR.

- If you have any reasonable doubts about the identity of the person making the request, you can ask for confirmation. For example, if the request comes from an unfamiliar email address, you can ask for photo ID.

- You can also ask the employee to clarify their request if you need help finding the data. They may already have said what systems, mailboxes or types of data they are interested in. If not, you can seek clarification. However, you cannot require them to narrow the request.

- When searching for relevant data, your duty is to carry out a reasonable and proportionate search. This has been confirmed by case law and guidance and has now been written into law by the DUA Act. You do not have to search every possible source. Instead, consider where relevant data is likely to be and how you can avoid creating large numbers of irrelevant results.

- Employees are only entitled to their own personal data. Other information can be redacted, especially if it is confidential or business sensitive and not about the employee.

- There are exemptions that allow you to withhold or redact certain data. For example, you should redact references to other people unless they have given permission or it is reasonable to disclose their identity. A person can be identifiable even if they are not named. For example, if an email says "another employee has repeatedly complained," and it is obvious who that is, you should redact it. You can also withhold legally privileged information, such as legal advice or documents prepared for legal proceedings.

- It is a criminal offence to delete or change data to avoid disclosing it.

To handle requests smoothly, map out a cradle-to-grave workflow. For example:

- When a request arrives, the recipient forwards it to a central mailbox that auto-generates a case number and acknowledgement. The acknowledgement, issued within two working days, confirms the statutory deadline and requests identity verification, if needed, setting the tone for a transparent process.

- The case handler meets the requester, if necessary and practical, to focus the scope without insisting on formal limitation (this can also be done via email). A simple conversation about the dates, projects or colleagues of most interest often removes large volumes of irrelevant data and speeds up delivery.

- Once the search parameters have been confirmed, the case handler issues targeted search instructions to mail and document management administrators, identifying which custodians' inboxes and network drives must be searched and which can be excluded on grounds of minimal relevance.

- After searches have been completed, focus on consolidation and review. Results are exported into review software or, in smaller organisations, a secure folder structure with consistent naming conventions. A reviewer works methodically, starting by identifying which documents contain personal data about the employee who has made the request. The reviewer then redacts third-party data and legally privileged material (as well as anything that is not personal data or is otherwise exempt) from those documents, recording each decision in an audit column so that, if challenged, you can explain the reasoning line by line. Where large attachments are repeated across emails, retain a single copy and link duplicates to cut volume.

- The final step is quality assurance. A second reviewer checks for missed redactions or over-redaction, then prepares the disclosure bundle, adding a short covering note that explains how to read the files and restates the individual's right to complain to the ICO. Delivering the bundle electronically in a password-protected archive reduces postage costs and allows delivery confirmation within the one-month limit.

Dealing with multiple DSARs

What if several employees submit DSARs at once? Handling one DSAR can be time-consuming. Dealing with several at the same time is even harder.

This is becoming more common. You might receive a wave of DSARs from individual employees or from a representative, such as a union or solicitor. The ICO has addressed this in its guidance. Each DSAR in a bulk request must be treated as a separate request, regardless of the extra work this creates.

Employers should remember:

- Each DSAR in a bulk request has the same legal status as a single request.

- The purpose of the request does not affect your duty to respond.

- If a third party makes the request, you should check that they are authorised to act for the employee.

- You should confirm the identity of the employee.

- Even if you do not hold any data on someone, you still need to respond to confirm this.

- You are expected to be prepared to deal with sudden increases in DSARs.

If someone complains to the ICO about how you handled a DSAR, the ICO will consider how many requests you received and what steps you took to respond. They will also take into account the company's size and resources, and are unlikely to take enforcement action if you have acted reasonably.

There is no exception that lets you ignore multiple DSARs received at once. Each one must still be dealt with. However, the ICO will be understanding if you have done your best and cannot meet every deadline. You should try to respond to each DSAR unless an exemption applies, such as when disclosure would reveal criminal activity or include third-party data that cannot be redacted.

The best way to comply is to act on each DSAR as it arrives. The deadline passes quickly, whether you have one month or an extension of three months. Check that the request is valid and whether any exemptions apply. Acknowledge receipt and give a rough date for your reply. If you need more details, ask for them early. Once you have the data, check for third-party references and either get consent or decide whether it is reasonable to share the data. If not, redact it.

Dealing with a 'lead' employee in a wave of DSARs

What if one or two employees encourage others to submit DSARs? Can you take disciplinary action?

You cannot discipline anyone simply for making a DSAR, as this is a legal right. If you decide to investigate the lead employee's actions, you must proceed with great care. Any disciplinary action must be based on something other than the DSAR itself. In theory, if the lead employee acts in a way that harms the business, there might be grounds for misconduct. But the reason must be very clear and must not relate to the DSAR itself.

There are a few practical steps you can take in this situation:

- Consider publishing an internal FAQ. This would not remove your duty to respond to each DSAR, but it might reduce the number of requests.

- Speak openly with employees. Acknowledge their legal rights, but explain the burden created by large numbers of DSARs. You might ask staff to hold off making requests while you manage the current volume.

- Get into a routine – you may find the process is less difficult than it first appears. You might find it easier to locate the data, create templates and even bring in temporary help. If you do hire a temp, make sure they sign a confidentiality agreement.

The right to rectification

Employees have the right to ask for their personal data to be corrected if it is inaccurate or incomplete.

You usually have to deal with this type of request within one month, though you can extend this if the request is complex or one of several made at once.

If you have shared the incorrect data with any third parties, you must tell them about the correction. You must also tell the employee who those third parties are.

The right of erasure (the 'right to be forgotten')

This right was widely talked about when the EU GDPR came into effect in 2018, but it is often misunderstood. It does not give employees a general right to have all their data deleted. The right only applies in specific situations, such as:

- Where the data is no longer needed for the original purpose

- Where the data was processed unlawfully, for example, if consent was invalid or the privacy notice was defective

- Where the processing is based on 'legitimate interests' and the employee objects, and you cannot show that your interests outweigh theirs

In an HR setting, this right will rarely apply to current employees because most of the data you hold will still be needed to manage the working relationship.

Still, all staff should know what a right to be forgotten request is and how to report it. This helps make sure that such requests are not missed and are handled properly.

As with rectification, if you erase any personal data under this right, you must tell any third parties you shared the data with that it has been deleted.

The right to restrict processing

Employees have a right to block or limit how their personal data is used in certain situations, including:

- When the employee disputes the accuracy of the data, and you need time to check it

- When the processing is unlawful, but the employee prefers restriction instead of deletion

- When you no longer need the data, but the employee needs it for a legal claim

- When you rely on 'legitimate interests' and the employee objects, while you assess whether your interests outweigh theirs

When processing is restricted, you can still store the data, but you cannot use it or make decisions based on it. The only exceptions are when the employee gives consent or when the data is needed for legal claims.

If you have shared the restricted data with others, you must inform them about the restriction.

Data portability

Employees can ask you to provide their personal data in a commonly used electronic format, either for themselves or for a third party. This right only applies if the lawful basis for processing is either consent or contractual necessity.

In the employment context, this is most likely to apply to data used to carry out your contractual duties. You must provide the data without charging a fee and without unnecessary delay.

Right to object

If you are using 'legitimate interests' as your basis for processing, the employee has the right to object if their personal situation gives them reason to believe their interests outweigh yours.

If they exercise this right, you must stop processing the data unless you can show that your grounds are more important than theirs, or the data is needed for legal claims.

Automated decision-making

Although this is described as a right, in practice, it works as a restriction. You must not make decisions that are fully automated and have legal or significant effects on a person unless it is necessary for a contract or the individual has given valid consent.

This is especially relevant now, with the growing use of AI in recruitment and employment processes.

'Wholly automated' means a decision made entirely by technology, without real human involvement. If a human has a final say, the decision may fall outside the restriction, but the involvement must be meaningful. A person simply signing off on a system's result without thinking it through will not count as genuine human input.

The rule only applies if the decision has a legal or similarly significant effect. This means the outcome must be more than minor. Examples include hiring decisions, pay rises or promotions.

To use wholly automated decision-making, one of the following must apply:

- The decision is necessary to carry out a contract or to take steps to enter into a contract at the individual's request
- The individual has given valid consent
- A law allows the decision to be made in this way

If you rely on any of these grounds, you must put safeguards in place.

This includes telling the individual about the logic behind the decision, giving them a way to express their views or challenge the decision and allowing for a human review of the decision.

When the DUA Act is implemented, the rules on automated decision-making will change. Under the changes, these rules will only apply where decisions are based wholly or partly on special category data. This will likely give employers more freedom to use AI and automated tools in recruitment and HR decisions. However, it is important to be aware that all other data protection law requirements will continue to apply, so employers will still need to (for example) identify and record an appropriate lawful basis, carry out a DPIA, and ensure transparency requirements are met, even if these decisions do not use special category data.

For more detail on AI and data protection, see Chapter 8.

Conclusion

As noted earlier, DSARs are by far the most commonly used right under the UK GDPR. Since the law came into effect, it has been relatively uncommon for employees to use any of the other rights, unless something unusual happens, such as concerns about biometric data or excessive monitoring.

Even so, it is important that all staff understand how to recognise any type of data rights request. That way, requests can be passed on quickly and handled properly within the tight deadlines set by the law.

Chapter 5

Sharing personal data

As HR professionals, you will often need to share employee personal data with third parties such as benefits providers, HMRC, future employers or the police. But personal data should not be shared freely or without thought. Even within your own organisation, you should carefully consider who actually needs access and put controls in place to manage that access.

Sharing data with third parties

When asked or required to share personal data with external parties, consider the following points:

- Is there a lawful basis for sharing? Sharing data is a form of processing, so you must identify a lawful basis before doing so. Sometimes, this will be straightforward; for example, you may have a legal duty to share data with HMRC, or you may need to share data with a benefits provider to fulfil your contract with the employee. Other times, you may need to carry out a legitimate interests assessment (see Chapter 2).

- Have you informed the employee, and do you need consent? You must consider whether your employee privacy notice already covers the data sharing and its purpose. If not, and if the sharing is for a new or unrelated purpose, you may need consent. However, there are some exemptions, such as where the data is shared for crime prevention, tax collection or legal proceedings, and informing the employee would undermine that purpose.

- Are you sharing only what is necessary? This is based on the principle of data minimisation. You should only share the data that is needed for the specific purpose. For example, if the police ask for all the data you hold about a former employee in order to contact them as a witness, they probably only need contact details. You are not legally obliged to share information with the police unless they have a court order or warrant.

- Are you sharing the data securely?
Personal data must always be shared securely. This could mean using password-protected files or a secure file-sharing platform.

- Do you need a data sharing agreement?
It is good practice to have a formal data sharing

agreement in place, especially where sharing happens regularly, for example, with insurers or benefit providers. The ICO's Data Sharing Code of Practice sets out what such agreements should include, such as roles, responsibilities, lawful bases and retention periods.

Sharing data with suppliers

The points above apply when you share data with third parties who are separate data controllers. But you may also need to share personal data with suppliers who act as data processors, meaning they process data on your behalf, following your instructions. You may work with legal or procurement teams on this, but there are still key responsibilities to be aware of:

- You must carry out due diligence. You are required to choose suppliers who can show they comply with data protection rules. This means checking what security and data handling processes they have in place. Larger suppliers may already have standard documentation for this. Make sure you read and understand it before signing anything.

- You must have certain contract terms in place. The UK GDPR requires specific clauses to be included in contracts between controllers and processors. These must explain what data will be processed, for what purpose and how the processor must handle it. Most suppliers will have their own contract terms. If you are a smaller organisation, your ability to negotiate may be limited. That said, processors do have direct legal duties under the UK GDPR, including on data security. If the processor suffers a security breach, and you have done your part, the responsibility will usually fall on them.

International transfers of personal data

Sometimes, sharing employee data with suppliers or other organisations will involve sending that data to another country. This comes with extra requirements. The rules are complex and subject to change, but the core principle is that personal data can only be transferred to a country outside the UK in three situations:

- The UK has a 'data bridge' with the country in question
- You can use 'appropriate safeguards'
- You can rely on an exemption

A data bridge, also known as an adequacy decision, means the UK government has decided that the country's legal system offers similar protection to UK data protection law. As of July 2025, the UK has data bridges in place for all EEA countries, as well as Switzerland, New Zealand, Andorra, Argentina, Uruguay, the Faroe Islands, Gibraltar, Jersey, Guernsey, the Isle of Man, Israel, Japan, South Korea, and Canada (private sector only).

There is also a limited data bridge with the United States. This applies only to US organisations that have signed up to the UK extension to the EU-US Data Privacy Framework (DPF). The US has historically presented challenges for data protection, particularly due to surveillance laws and limited rights for non-US citizens. For now, registration with the DPF is considered sufficient, but this area is under constant review and may change.

'Appropriate safeguards' allow you to share data even without a data bridge. The most common are standard contractual clauses (SCCs), or, within corporate groups, binding corporate rules (BCRs).

BCRs are internal data sharing policies used within multinational groups. They must be approved by the ICO, take time to implement and are not widely used.

SCCs are much more common. In the UK, they take the form of the International Data Transfer Agreement (IDTA), which can be used for transfers to any country outside the UK. If your organisation operates in both the UK and the EU, you can use the EU's SCCs along with the ICO's UK Addendum to cover transfers from both jurisdictions without signing two separate contracts.

However, using BCRs or SCCs is not enough on its own. Since the Court of Justice of the EU (CJEU) case of *Schrems II* (Case C-311/18) in 2020, you must also carry out a transfer risk assessment (TRA).

This means assessing whether the laws in the destination country allow the recipient to comply with the terms of the SCCs or IDTA.

A TRA is often viewed as purely legal, yet in practice, it is a multidisciplinary exercise that HR must be involved in whenever employee personal data is transferred to a third country (for example, if payroll, benefits or employee experience platforms are hosted offshore). A robust TRA can be framed in five stages.

1. **Scoping:** Identify the specific categories of personal data that will leave the UK, the exact processing operations performed abroad, and the suppliers and sub-processors involved. Creating a flow diagram can help you to visualise exposures.

2. **Destination analysis:** Draw on open sources (such as UK government human-rights reports and reputable law-firm briefings) to summarise the legal regime of the destination country, focussing on surveillance powers, redress mechanisms and any known precedents of disproportionate state access.

3. **Risk assessment:** Consider the risk level of the transfers, based on factors like the sensitivity and volume of data, and the frequency of transfers. For example, payroll data sent weekly to a

processor in Bangalore containing NI numbers and bank details is inherently higher risk than anonymised engagement-survey scores. Use a scored questionnaire so HR and IT can supply facts quickly.

4. **Supplementary measures selection:** If there is a risk that the destination country's legal regime prevents the recipient from complying with the IDTA, you will need to put in place supplementary measures to protect the data and mitigate that risk. Technical measures may include end-to-end encryption, with decryption keys retained in the UK, and organisational measures could be contractual audit rights or rapid breach notification clauses.

5. **Decision and record-keeping:** Compile the TRA report, obtain sign-off from the DPO and, where high residual risk remains, escalate to the board. File the TRA alongside the IDTA and note the review date (usually annually or when the processing changes).

Embedding this workflow in your supplier onboarding checklist ensures that international transfers never proceed without a clear, documented risk-based justification.

The ICO has issued practical guidance and a TRA tool to help organisations assess risk. The ICO's approach focuses on the nature of the data and the risks posed by the transfer. If the data being transferred is low risk, the TRA may be relatively straightforward. However, if you are also subject to EU rules, the process may be stricter. The EU has taken a more rigid approach, so joint UK-EU transfers may require more analysis.

If there is no data bridge and you cannot use appropriate safeguards, you might still be able to rely on an exemption. These exemptions (called derogations) include situations where the employee has given consent, the transfer is needed to perform a contract, or the transfer is part of a legal claim.

However, these exemptions should only be used for occasional, low-risk transfers. They are not meant for routine or repeated transfers and should not be relied on as a long-term solution.

Chapter 6

Employee monitoring

Employee monitoring is nothing new. Employers have long used tools like timesheets, punch cards, CCTV and performance checklists. But advances in technology, alongside the increase in home and remote working after COVID-19, have led many employers to monitor staff more closely. They may want to confirm that employees are working as expected, especially when not in the office.

While it is understandable for employers to want to keep an eye on employee activity, monitoring can be highly intrusive and must be done with care.

The ICO has published detailed guidance on worker monitoring as part of its *Employment Practices and Data Protection* resources. The guidance is worth reading to understand what is expected.

One recent example of high-profile activity in this space involved the ICO issuing an enforcement notice to Serco, which had used facial recognition technology to clock employees in and out. During lockdown, the BBC also reported on a business owner who used software to track hours, keystrokes, mouse activity, and websites visited, and even took regular screenshots of employees' screens.

All of these monitoring methods involve processing personal data. If you are considering monitoring, here are some key points to think about.

First, ask whether a less intrusive method could achieve the same goal. This should always be a starting point. You need to consider alternatives with less impact on privacy. If you go ahead with the monitoring, you must be clear about why those alternatives are not suitable. In the Serco case, the company tried to justify facial recognition by saying employees were sharing access cards, but it could not provide evidence or show why a less intrusive method would not have worked.

Second, identify your lawful basis for processing the data. You should assess and record this, using a legitimate interests assessment (LIA) if required. If you are using biometric data, like facial or fingerprint recognition, you will also need an additional condition under Article 9 of the UK GDPR. Most legal bases and conditions require the processing to be "necessary". If what you are doing is excessive, or there are less invasive ways to achieve the same result, you are unlikely to meet this test.

Third, you must inform employees. Covert monitoring is rarely justifiable. Transparency is essential. You need to tell employees what monitoring is happening, why and how the data will be used.

Fourth, employees must have a choice in some situations. If you rely on legitimate interests, the employee has the right to object.

Fifth, consider what the impact of the monitoring will be. If you are reviewing office access data in general to plan for when to stock the kitchen, that is low risk. But using the same data to take disciplinary action against employees for failure to attend the office often enough is more serious and harder to justify.

Many organisations find it helpful to translate those points into a lightweight 'monitoring protocol' so that managers cannot introduce new tools by stealth. A workable protocol starts with a purpose statement, for instance, "to verify attendance and support resource planning, not to judge productivity minute by minute".

It then sets clear boundaries, for example: data must not be used to make disciplinary decisions without additional evidence, keystroke logging is prohibited, and screenshots are captured no more than once every ten minutes.

Before any monitoring begins, a protocol may then require project sponsors to complete a short form giving details of the monitoring, and to carry out an LIA and, where the processing is high-risk, a DPIA. A good deal of employee monitoring activity is likely to require a DPIA. The form may ask them to specify retention periods (for example, for access card data, thirty days may well be adequate) and nominate a data steward responsible for deletion. HR and the DPO jointly review the form within ten working days, ensuring pace without rubber-stamping.

The protocol may then enable transparency to be delivered through a layered approach: for example, an intranet FAQ explaining what is collected, a banner on login reminding employees that the system is active, and a longer policy available on request. Crucially, employees are offered a channel to raise concerns anonymously, which not only satisfies fairness obligations but also often surfaces configuration issues early.

Finally, governance cannot end at deployment. The protocol should deal with ongoing governance. For example, at least quarterly, the data steward exports a sampling report, showing who has accessed monitoring data, why and whether action was taken. HR reviews the report and flags any drift from the original justification, such as line managers using screenshots to evaluate performance contrary to the protocol. By institutionalising this cycle (proposal, assessment, transparency, oversight), HR demonstrates accountability and keeps monitoring proportionate to genuine business needs.

The more intrusive your monitoring, the harder it is to justify. You must show that your approach is fair and proportionate. In most cases, a DPIA will be needed. DPIAs are a useful way to identify risks and show compliance. As part of a DPIA, you may also want to consult with employees or unions. This can help identify issues early and avoid future disputes.

Chapter 7

AI and biometrics

It would be hard to write about data protection in 2025 without covering AI. Since the explosion of generative AI in late 2022, many organisations have adopted or are exploring AI tools. For some, AI is now part of everyday operations.

AI offers many opportunities in HR. Examples include using generative AI to draft job descriptions, chatbots that help employees find policy information, systems that let employees update details or book holidays, AI tools that transcribe and summarise interviews, programs that match CVs to job criteria, and biometric attendance systems. There are also more advanced tools, like emotion recognition software which assesses customer service interactions, and "agentic AI" solutions are starting to emerge, which automate end-to-end processes like complaints handling. Tools like Microsoft Copilot and Google Gemini are also being rolled out widely across organisations.

The UK GDPR applies regardless of the technology being used. This means that AI must meet the same rules as any other form of personal data processing. However, AI does raise particular issues and risks that HR teams need to consider.

If you use AI to process personal data, especially in a new or unusual way, you almost certainly need to carry out a DPIA. You must also consider how transparent you are about the use of AI. You do not need to notify staff every time AI is involved, but where AI is used to process personal data for new purposes, or where it collects or infers new personal data, you must be clear about it. If you use AI to make decisions without human involvement, you must also be able to explain how the decision was made (see Chapter 5). This can be difficult if the supplier is reluctant to share details of how their system works.

You also need a clear lawful basis for the processing. This is about the purpose of the processing, not the fact that AI is involved. However, using AI may shift the balance of interests between you and the employee. In some cases, you may need to offer a non-AI alternative. The overall principle of fairness remains important. Your use of AI must be ethical.

Accuracy is another concern. Generative AI does not always produce reliable outputs. There have already been well-known examples where people were falsely declared dead or wrongly linked to scandals. If you use AI to summarise an interview and it incorrectly records that a candidate had been a bully, that could lead to legal claims if the candidate is rejected based on that information. Bias is also a major risk. Amazon scrapped a recruitment tool in 2015 after it was found to discriminate against women. For these reasons, testing and human review are essential.

You must also think about purpose limitation. AI suppliers often want to use the personal data you provide to help train or improve their tools. This could go beyond what is covered in your privacy notice and might require employee consent. Consider whether you are happy for suppliers to use personal data in this way and whether it is appropriate to allow it.

Most HR teams buy in AI systems rather than build them. This means you are dependent on suppliers for compliance support. Ask suppliers questions about how the tool works, how it was trained, what testing was done and how they manage its accuracy. You also need a strong contract with clear data protection clauses.

Responsible AI use is not just about following data protection rules. The UK government introduced five principles in 2023 to guide AI regulation:

1. Safety, security and robustness

2. Appropriate transparency and explainability

3. Fairness

4. Governance and accountability

5. Contestability and redress.

These overlap with UK GDPR concepts but go further. Other laws and rules may apply too.

To manage this properly, organisations should set up internal governance for AI. This means creating policies, procedures, training and clear ways of assessing risk before using AI tools or signing contracts with AI vendors.

The ICO has excellent guidance on AI and data protection, including in recruitment. It is worth reading to understand what is expected. Because AI raises risks beyond data protection, this is one area where legal advice may be especially valuable.

Chapter 8

Conclusion

There is a lot to consider when managing data protection in HR, but it does not have to be overly complex. These five key steps can help make compliance part of everyday practice:

1. Build data protection into your workplace culture through regular training that fits your sector and organisation.

2. Carry out regular checks on your UK GDPR compliance and update your policies when needed.

3. Make sure your privacy notices for employees, workers and candidates are clear, complete and easy to understand.

4. Only collect the data you genuinely need, and regularly review your processes to avoid gathering unnecessary information.

5. Stay up to date with guidance from the ICO, especially anything focused on HR. Keeping an eye on enforcement action can also help you understand the regulator's current priorities and avoid potential issues.

With these steps in place, you can make data protection a routine part of your HR processes and reduce the risk of mistakes.

Appendix A

UK GDPR compliance checklist

☐ We have recorded details of our HR data processing activities in central records of processing.

☐ We have an internal data protection policy that tells employees what their data protection obligations are and how they should ensure compliance.

☐ We have identified a lawful basis for all our HR data processing activities and a processing condition for any special category data or criminal conviction and offence data we process.

☐ We have a privacy notice in place for employees, other workers and candidates to enable them to understand how we process their personal data.

☐ We make sure we only collect the data we actually need for the purposes for which it is collected.

☐ We have, and enforce, a data retention policy to ensure we don't keep personal data for longer than we need it.

☐ We limit access to personal data to only those who need it for their roles.

☐ We have procedures in place to comply with data subject rights requests.

☐ We don't carry out wholly automated decision-making with legal or significant effects unless it is necessary for a contract or we have consent.

☐ We ensure that personal data we process is appropriately secure.

☐ We have procedures in place for sharing personal data in response to requests from third parties or pursuant to ongoing arrangements.

☐ We ensure suppliers who process personal data for us are subject to due diligence and robust contractual requirements.

☐ We have training in place for all employees on their data protection obligations, and we monitor completion.

☐ We ensure that DPIAs are carried out for all high-risk data processing activities, including employee monitoring activities and the use of AI and biometric systems.

TLT

Legal advice to navigate you through the risks

We're your business advisers as well as your lawyers, working in step with you to protect your interests today and progress your ambitions for tomorrow.

With local, national and international reach, we draw on our diverse expertise to find solutions and look ahead to create opportunities for what comes next.

- Digital
- Financial services
- Future energy
- Leisure, food and drink
- Government & public services
- Real estate
- Retail & consumer goods

tlt.com

Also by
Daniel Barnett

Available on Amazon
or visit
go.danielbarnett.com/books

JOIN DANIEL EVERY SATURDAY EVENING AT
9PM WHEN HE PRESENTS THE

LBC Legal Hour
— OR CATCH UP VIA THE GLOBAL PLAYER,
AT bit.ly/lbclegalhour

SATURDAYS, 9PM

Dear HR Professional,

I take my hat off to you.

Having supported the HR community for so many years, I know It's a challenging job you do, sometimes under really difficult circumstances.

The tricky HR issues you have to handle must take up a tremendous amount of your time, your energy and your brain power. I bet it can be exhausting for you to work under that level of pressure.

Being An HR Professional In Today's Business Environment Is TOUGH!

Maintaining your high standards of professionalism must be a real struggle, especially when your efforts and expertise often go unappreciated.

I'll wager you have to make decisions on challenging HR situations you've sometimes never encountered before. Even if you're part of a team, it must sometimes feel like you're working in isolation.

With so much complexity and ambiguity, do you ever find you're not clear whether you're doing the right thing when there's so much to think about?

I expect it can be draining too. You've got to make tough decisions which may be unpopular.

The pressure's on you to ensure people are treated fairly while the business complies with its legal obligations.

It's a thankless task, especially if you've got grief coming at you from all sides.

Doubt can creep in too. Even though you're an extremely competent professional, you might even begin to question yourself...What if you've got it wrong?

You've got to cope with all that, whilst constantly having to convince any doubting stakeholders you're adding value to the business.

That pressure must take its toll on you.

You wouldn't be human if it didn't cause you tension, stress or even worse!

Being the caring professional you are, I bet you often take work home with you.

If You're Not Careful The Stress WILL Creep Up On You

And I don't just mean opening your laptop on your couch when everyone else is watching Eastenders.

We all know of families and relationships that come a poor second to the pressures and challenges faced at work.

Yours too..?

But does it have to be that way?

Should you feel the responsibility of the HR world is entirely on your shoulders and that you've got to bear that burden alone?

The answer is a firm no.

It doesn't have to be like that.

There Is An Answer To Help Make Your Work & Your Life Much Easier For You

There's a place you can get all the help, support, advice and encouragement you need to ease the constant pressure you have to bear.

IT'S CALLED THE HR INNER CIRCLE.

It will lift the burden you're carrying by giving you swift access to comprehensive resources and live practical guidance you can implement right away.

It's information I know will save you time, energy and effort.

It's a vibrant, active community of caring, like minded HR professionals willing to help you.

There are resources packed full of practical, actionable advice for you that's difficult to find anywhere else.

And it doesn't matter what you're working on.

Whether it be workforce engagement, attracting and keeping talent, diversity and inclusion or employee health and well being, you'll find support for all of that.

You're covered even if you're working on one of those tricky, sensitive, people problems you never see coming until they land squarely on your plate.

Timely Support To Make Your Job Easier, Can Be Rapidly Found In The HR Inner Circle

As a member of the HR Inner Circle, to get the support you want…

…just ask.

Your first port of call is the vibrant Facebook group, bursting at the seams with incredible HR professionals like you.

Just post your question and let it bubble and simmer in the collective genius of the group.

By the end of the day, you'll have at least 3-5 comments on your post, often more.

You'll get relevant, insightful and practical guidance that comes from the hard earned experience of your fellow members.

Often you'll get a response within a couple of hours. Sometimes you'll get an answer within minutes - even if it's late in the evening!

This highly active community never fails to astound me with just how willing they are to help fellow HR professionals like you.

They readily and generously share their hard earned knowledge and experience.

You Can Get Answers From Real People Quickly AND From Our Extensive Resource Library Too

...really important for someone working on their own who needs to check things out, or just bounce a few ideas around.

- Quentin Colborn
Director, QC People Management Ltd

While you wait for a response from the Facebook group, you'll likely find answers in the resource-rich members' vault on our secure online portal as well.

It takes just 2 clicks and a quick keyword search using our Rapid Results Search Tool.

You'll instantly find precisely where your topic is covered in our extensive back catalogue of monthly magazines and audio seminars.

In under 30 seconds you can find exactly what you're after.

It's that quick and easy.

…And if you need a specific legal insight?

Then pose your question live to an expert employment lawyer in our monthly Q&A session.

It'll either be me or one of my prominent contemporaries. You'll get your answer immediately without having to pay any legal costs.

If you can't wait, you'll find where it's been answered before with a quick search of previous Q&A sessions.

Our clever index system means you can find a question, and in a single click get straight to the recorded answer.

But perhaps you need to dive deep and explore the different options open to you to solve a particularly tricky problem?

Then join one of our monthly HR Huddles. There you can run your specific situation past other HR professionals.

They'll offer their insights, share their experience and work WITH you to find a solution that works FOR you.

You'll find all of this in one convenient place - the HR Inner Circle.

I've spent years practising law and have become recognised as one of the UK's leading employment law barristers. I've even got my own radio show!

It's Been A Labour Of Love Putting The HR Inner Circle Together So It Works For Professionals Like You

It's great to see that we all experience tricky cases from time to time.

- Annabelle Carey
Managing Consultant,
HR Services Partnership

But more importantly for you, I've also developed another skill.

It's bringing useful employment expertise AND practical experience together in a way that supports busy, overworked (and sometimes stressed) HR professionals like you.

Everything you're likely to need is **literally at your fingertips.**

This will save you time, energy and effort.

Being a member also means your business and clients will see you as even MORE INFORMED about the intricacies of employment law.

They'll marvel at how well you keep up to date when you're busy working so hard for them.

You'll be seen making quicker decisions and implementing effective solutions to accelerate the growth of the organisation.

You'll make impressive time and cost savings for the business.

And those tricky, off-piste situations you've never come across before..?

Well, nothing will faze you, because you're backed up by an HR support system second to none.

But more importantly, you'll feel that pressure gently ease off.

With the relief you'll feel knowing that such great help and guidance is just a few minutes, you'll wonder how you survived without it!

Here's what you get when you join the HR Inner Circle:

That's Why I'm Inviting You To Join And Reap The Many Rewards Of Membership

WWW.HRINNERCIRCLE.CO.UK

Benefit #1 - you'll get unlimited access to the hugely popular HR Inner Circle Facebook Private Group

- Tap into the vast wealth of knowledge, experience, insight and wisdom of the top 0.5% of your profession at any time, day or night.

- In less than 5 minutes you can post ANY HR question and get insightful answers and suggestions in a couple of hours or less, from some of the best in your profession.

- Fast track your impact by discovering effective shortcuts and workarounds from HR people who've been "there" and done "it".

- Expand and deepen your network of like minded individuals, secure in the knowledge they're as dedicated and as ambitious as you.

- Increase your prestige with your colleagues and stakeholders by being part of such an exclusive and prominent HR community.

- Gain confidence in your judgment and decisions by using the highly responsive community as a sounding board for your ideas.

Benefit #2 - you'll receive 11 copies of the HR Inner Circular Magazine every year

- Enjoy that satisfying "THUD" on your door mat every month when the postman delivers your very own copy of the HR Inner Circular magazine.

- Quickly discover exactly what the law says about key issues affecting HR professionals around the UK like you.

- Get concise and practical guidance on how employment law applies to the challenging situations and circumstances you deal with every day.

- Avoid the mistakes of others by applying the lessons from the in depth analysis of real life case studies.

- Benefit from a legal deep dive by the UK's leading employment law barrister into a topical employment question posed by a fellow member (perhaps you!).

- Review a summary of recent important Facebook Group discussions worthy of sharing, that you may have missed.

- Explore a range of related and relevant topics useful for your practice and your broader professional development.

The magazine is really informative, the Facebook group such a community, and I think exceptional value for money.

- Lis Moore
Head of Advisory & Support Services,
Society of Local Council Clerks

Benefit #3 - Monthly Audio Seminars

- A 60 minute legal deep dive by me into an important subject relevant to you and your practice.

- Professionally recorded content recorded exclusively for the HR Inner Circle - you'll not find this information anywhere else.

- Carefully structured content that's easy to consume, understand and apply in your work as an HR professional.

- Episodes delivered every month so you can stay current on the latest issues affecting HR professionals.

- The convenience of listening to the recording online or downloading the mp3 for later enjoyment at a time suitable to your busy schedule (perfect for any commute).

Benefit #4 - you get an exclusive invite to a live online Q&A Session every fortnight, led by an expert employment lawyer

- Gain 60 minutes of live and direct access to the sharpest legal minds from my secret little black book of contacts.

- Get answers to your knottiest employment law questions, and solutions to your trickiest HR problems, from some of the brightest employment lawyers in the UK.

- Avoid having to pay the £300-£400 it would cost you to ask a lawyer your question outside of the HR Inner Circle.

- Benefit from valuable insights from the answers given to other members.

- If you can't attend live, watch the recording when it's convenient for you.

- Quickly access the recorded answer to any question asked in the session by simply clicking the question index for that session.

- Save time by downloading the session transcription to scan-read at a time suitable for you.

Benefit #5 - join a live Monthly Huddle with other HR Professionals to solve your most challenging HR problems

- Attend your very own mini-mastermind group of highly qualified, highly regarded and experienced fellow HR professionals to "group think" through an issue you're facing right now.

- Develop bespoke solutions to the unique problems and challenges you have to deal with in a safe, supportive and confidential environment.

- Feel safe knowing these online zoom calls are NOT recorded to respect the sensitivity of issues addressed and the privacy of those involved. [NOTE - a professional transcriber attends and takes written notes. An anonymised summary is then made available to the membership]

- Recent Huddle topics included changing employee benefits, mandatory vaccination, career breaks, sickness during disciplinaries, effective worker forums and hybrid working arrangements.

Benefit #6 - access our Templates & Resources Centre

- Gain immediate access to our library of the most popular and frequently used forms, assessments, agreements, checklists, letter templates, questionnaires and reports to help the busiest HR professionals save time and get things done quicker and easier.

- Download them as Word documents, so you can edit and personalise them to fit your business needs

- New templates added every single month

Benefit #7 - build your own Employment Law Library

- We send you several brand-new books on employment law several times each year

- Acquire your own physical library of concise, easy-to-read and fully updated textbooks

- Recent titles include Hiring Staff, Managing Sickness Absence, Spotting Malingering and Resolving Grievances

Benefit #8 - free Ticket to our Annual Conference

- The perfect opportunity to extend your personal network of fellow HR professionals.

- Meet up face to face with the people who've been supporting you in the Facebook Group and HR Huddles so you can deepen those connections even further.

- Gather key insights and takeaways to help you personally and professionally from some of the best speakers on the circuit. Previous speakers have covered motivation, dealing with difficult people, goal setting and productivity, decision making and social media marketing.

- Get instant access to recordings of all previous conferences so even if you can't attend in person, you can benefit from the event in your own time.

- Includes probably the best conference lunch you'll ever have - a bold claim I know, but we use outstanding caterers.

It never ceases to amaze me the amount of time and effort people put into the Facebook group, sharing their experiences, advice, and sage words of wisdom.

- Emma Lister
HR Consultant, SME HR Services

Benefit #9 - your Personal Concierge will help you get the best out of your membership

- You get personal access to Nina who'll point you in the direction of exactly where to find what you need. She's supported hundreds of members over the 5 years she's been part of the team.

- Nina also works closely with the 11 back office staff that support the operation. In the extremely unlikely event she doesn't know where something is, she knows who will.

HOW MUCH DOES JOINING THE HR INNER CIRCLE COST?

There's no doubt in my mind the annual value of membership benefits is in the many thousands of pounds range.

But you're not going to pay anywhere near that. Let me remind you of what that small monthly fee gives you every year

Access to the private Facebook Group	INCLUDED
HR Inner Circular Magazine subscription	INCLUDED
Monthly Audio Seminars	INCLUDED
Live Q&A sessions	INCLUDED
Monthly HR Huddles	INCLUDED
Templates & Resources Centre	INCLUDED
Employment Law Library	INCLUDED
Free ticket to the HR Inner Circle Annual Conference	INCLUDED
Your Personal Membership Concierge	INCLUDED

TOTAL   PRICELESS

Another way of looking at your investment is this:

Because access to what you need is so quick…

Join today and that price is fixed for as long as you remain a member. You'll always pay the same, even if we increase the price to new members (which we regularly do).

…it's like having your very own part time, legally trained, assistant HR Business Partner, just waiting to provide you with all the answers you need…

WWW.HRINNERCIRCLE.CO.UK

Plus, With Membership Of The HR Inner Circle, You'll Also Get These 4 Additional Resources For FREE!

Additional Resource #1 - Handling Awkward Conversations

A video case study masterclass you can share with managers to train them to handle awkward staff disciplinary, performance and attitude problems. A huge time saver for you.

Additional Resource #2 - 6 x HR Employment Online Courses

Immediate, on demand access to six thorough, online HR courses (with more constantly added), including Employment Tribunal Compensation, Chat GPT for HR Professionals, Deconstructing TUPE, Changing Terms & Conditions, Unconscious Bias At Work and Handling Grievances.

Additional Resource #3 - Free listing on the Register of Investigators

Advertise your professional investigations service in our member's portal.

Additional Resource #4 - Significant discounts on sets of policies, contracts, and other courses.

Get member discounts on my Getting Redundancy Right and HR Policies products as well as other price reductions as new products are released.

WWW.HRINNERCIRCLE.CO.UK

It's a really good investment. The support you get from other Facebook group members is fantastic. Whatever your question, someone will know the answer. Access to Daniel's experience and knowledge through the podcasts and Q&A is invaluable too.

- Tracy Madgwick
HR Consultant, Crafnant HR

I'm So Confident Joining The HR Inner Circle Is The Right Decision For You, Here's My

NO LIMITS

GUARANTEE

Take action and join the HR Inner Circle **now**.

If you're not 100% satisfied with your investment, you can cancel at ANY time.

Just tell us, and your membership will end immediately. No long-term contracts. No notice periods. No fuss.

I'm comfortable doing this because I know once you join, you'll find the support, the information and the strategies so useful, you'll never want to leave.

Before you decide though, let me be very clear about membership of the HR Inner Circle.

It's only for ambitious and dedicated HR professionals who want to accelerate and increase their impact by plugging into an HR ecosystem with its finger firmly on the pulse of what's working right now in HR.

If you're just plodding along and are content with just getting by, then this is probably not for you.

But if you're drawn to benefiting from standing shoulder to shoulder with some of the giants in the HR community who will help you solve your toughest problems, then joining the HR Inner Circle is the RIGHT decision for you.

Join here now:

WWW.HRINNERCIRCLE.CO.UK

Daniel Barnett

P.S. Remember when you join you get unrestricted access to the private Facebook group, the monthly magazine delivered direct to your door, the monthly audio seminar, regular free books, templates, checklists and resources, on-demand video courses, over 100 audio seminars and back copies of magazines, live interactive Q&A sessions with a lawyer, focused monthly huddles with other HR professionals, a free ticket to the annual conference, your personal concierge plus a bunch of additional resources…